Everyman's Poetry

Everyman, I will go with thee,
and be thy guide

Into a Towering Passion

Poems on Love

Selected and edited by A. D. P. BRIGGS

EVERYMAN

J. M. Dent · London

This edition published by Everyman Paperbacks in 2000
Selection, introduction and other critical apparatus
© J. M. Dent 2000

J. M. Dent
Orion Publishing Group
Orion House
5 Upper St Martin's Lane
London WC2H 9EA

Typeset by Deltatype Ltd, Birkenhead, Merseyside
Printed in Great Britain by
The Guernsey Press Co. Ltd, Guernsey, C.I.

British Library Cataloguing-in-Publication
Data is available on request

ISBN 0 460 88204 X

Contents

Note on the Editor

A. D. P. BRIGGS, formerly Professor of Russian at Birmingham University, is a specialist in modern Russian literature, mainly of the nineteenth century, and in European poetry. He has written ten books, five of them on Alexander Pushkin. His editions of Pushkin, FitzGerald's *Omar Khayyam*, English Sonnets and Shakespeare's Love Poetry have already appeared in the Everyman's Poetry series.

Introduction

Love is a circle that doth restless move
In the same sweet eternity of love

Robert Herrick

A Glory Circling Round the Soul

This grand phrase of Byron's ('Love') may sound excessive as a description of love, but its extravagance is understandable. Love is the biggest of all human subjects. Our lives are tiny, death is intractable and God seems far away. Of all the great ideas that dominate our existence only Love can be embraced as immediate and understandable as well as being elemental and eternal. There is nothing more important in a human life.

Love takes many forms, but for the purpose of this small collection we are considering Eros rather than Agape, amorous sexual relations rather than selfless devotion to other people. Behind Eros lies biology. The reproduction of our species is our primary function, and we animals need to bring male and female together with some urgency and frequency so that fertilised eggs are implanted in wombs and new human beings produced. But this is sexual attraction, not love. Why do we need love? Again, it is a matter of biology. Our astonishingly powerful brains, each containing as many neurons as there are stars in the Milky Way, need a long period for careful development, before and after birth. The human child, busily accommodating vast amounts of information and above all learning language, needs parental protection over several years before it can stand alone in the world. With this in mind, natural selection has favoured the creation of a strong bond between parents, thus increasing the chances of their mutual devotion over the necessary span. That invisible bond is love, and it holds human affairs together like gravity binding the universe.

In the earliest days of civilisation, when art and ritual grew into human experience, fertility seems to have vied for pre-eminence with hunting and warfare. In less violent modern times, however, love has emerged as one of the most important cultural preoccupations. In some genres it has come to enjoy massive pre-eminence. Literature, and especially lyric poetry, is one such area. If you glance through the index of *The Oxford Dictionary of Quotations* you will be able to take a rough measure of how strongly this subject predominates. Look up 'Life' and 'Live' and you will find about eight hundred entries. 'God' will yield about the same, and 'Heaven' will add half as many again. 'Death' and 'Dead' are about equal to God and Life. But when you come to 'Love' (and cognates) you will find column after tall column, more than four pages of tiny print amounting to about 1,300 references. 'Heart' will also account for nearly as many allusions as God, Life and Death. Add Heart and Love together and you have almost two thousand entries, a much bigger proportion than any other subject could hope to claim.

The Secret of the Sun

Love as a literary subject is massive and complex. At its most lurid the force is seen by the poets as something of transcendent power, sometimes as mighty as the universe itself. Robert Bridges views our world as a creation of love, and love itself as the unique means of understanding the universe in macro- and microcosm:

> Love can tell, and love alone,
> Whence the million stars were strewn,
> Why each atom knows its own . . .
> ('My delight and thy delight')

Earlier he has claimed that 'Love . . . Hath the secret of the sun', all of which seems like a genuine attempt to relate humanity to the cosmos through poetry. This is not usually the case. More commonly a poet, smitten by the full force of love, will be so fired with enthusiasm that only hyperbole will suffice to express such powerful feelings. Thus Robbie Burns will profess himself capable of loving 'till a' the seas gang dry' and 'the rocks melt wi' the sun' ('A Red, Red Rose'). Elizabeth Barrett Browning (translating from the Portuguese) loves 'to the depth and breadth and height /[Her] soul can reach, when feeling out of sight/ For the ends of Being . . .' ('How do I love thee? Let me count the ways'). John Ruskin claims that Sun and Breath may fail, but never his love ('Trust thou thy love . . .'); and Robert Southey describes his love, which descends from heaven and shall return there, as 'indestructible' ('Love Cannot Die').

The mention of heaven is instructive. If not the cosmos, then divinity is frequently invoked as the only metaphor large enough to convey the truth of love. Byron describes it as 'A feeling from the Godhead caught' ('Love'); Campion compares his mistress's face to a heavenly paradise and her eyes to watching angels ('There is a garden in her face'); Hopkins, inviting God to a wedding, sees the lovers as bound to each other by divine charity 'deeper than divined' ('At the Wedding March'); Thomas D'Urfey, while insisting on Chloe's physicality, still compares her to a saint and a goddess and calls her divine in the last word of his poem ('Chloe Divine'). For good measure, though, we should note that two and a half centuries ago William Cartwright dismissed this sort of thing as 'thin love' and called back down to earth those 'that tread Those vain aerial ways' with a reminder that love dwells in the body more than the spirit ('No Platonic Love'). Bodily love, much celebrated in poetry, is a subject we shall return to.

The Cruel Madness of Love

The course of love cannot be expected ever to run smooth. It causes as much anguish as delight. Tennyson despaired of it, putting these sardonic words into the mouth of the narrator of 'Maud':

> And most of all would I flee from the cruel madness of love,
> The honey of poison-flowers and all the measureless ill.

For every joyous love poem there is one of agony. Love is a tantalising dream ('A Report Song in a Dream, Between a Shepherd and His Nymph'), a sickness, torment and tempest ('Love is a sickness . . .'), a bleeding wound ('Red and White Roses'), sweetness turned to bitterness ('Grown and Flown'), a painful, unspoken secret ('I hid my love . . .'), an affliction worse than blindness ('Cards and Kisses'), an absence leading to grief and death ('The Solitary Lyre'), a smarting pain that can be assuaged only by sleep or death. It is irrational ('Love's Logic') and chancy ('And if I did what then?'). It is elusive and complicated, infuriating and uncontrollable. Worst of all, once attained it is likely to dissolve rapidly and disappear. At least a quarter of the poems in this book will complain that love is too short-lived to provide lasting satisfaction. Why should this be so?

For one thing, death used to intervene between lovers, removing one of them prematurely. Many sad phrases adorn the following pages, marking the early passing of a loved one. The young woman asks: 'What is this/ Lieth there so cold?' in Bret Harte's poem ('What the Bullet Sang'). Hardy addresses a mournful poem to a 'Woman much missed' ('The Voice'). 'She pass'd away like morning dew', complains Hartley Coleridge ('Early Death'). William Broome asserts that 'Time destroys what Sickness spares' ('The Rosebud'), and Dante Gabriel Rossetti uses stilletto monosyllables to inform us of his tragedy: 'And she is hence, and I am here' ('A Death-Parting').

All too often it is not the lover, but love itself, that dies. Sir Walter Ralegh tells us bleakly that neither youth nor love can last ('Her Reply'). Contemplating 'the end of a summer day', William Allingham declares that 'Sweet Love [is] dead' ('An Evening'). 'Love is dead', agrees John Ford, but there is worse to come: 'Love's martyrs must be ever, ever dying' ('Oh no more, no more, too late'). George Meredith explains further: love can never last because of human frailty.

> Here is a fitting spot to dig Love's grave . . .
> We are betray'd by what is false within.
> ('Love's Grave')

The death of love can often be anticipated. Not infrequently an inconstant partner loves and leaves, showing no shame for his casual behaviour. The Rover bids 'Adieu for evermore' with scarcely a backward glance in Sir Walter Scott's poem ('The Rover's Adieu'). More eloquent but equally cynical is Ernest Dowson's lover; well into his next affair but thinking back to the one before, he claims to be 'desolate and sick of an old passion' and swears that 'I have been faithful to thee, Cynara! in my fashion' ('Non Sum Qualis Eram Bonae Sub Regno Cynarae'). Sir George Etherege is little more tactful, merely suggesting that it is better to get on with the business of loving than wonder too much how long the thrill may last ('To a Lady Asking Him How Long He Would Love Her'). In a poem with the ironic title 'The Constant Lover', the hero is shocked at his own fidelity, having 'loved/ Three whole days together'; his current love should thank her lucky stars that she has held on to him for so long, when he might have had a 'dozen dozen' others. Thomas Campbell explains why inconstancy happens, in his poem, 'Freedom and Love', which links these two conditions inextricably. 'Love's a fire that needs renewal . . .', he proposes, looking on these things with a masculine eye, and continuing in the same vein:

> Love's wing moults when caged and captured,
> Only free, he soars enraptured.

According to Sir Thomas Wyatt women can be just as capricious. In words addressed to his ex-lover's next mate he warns that her protestations of love have been heard before by others '(Quondam was I in my lady's grace'). It needed another woman to restore some sobriety to this subject; Emily Brontë acknowledges that love is so unreliable, like a rose fading in the autumn, that we should place our trust in the evergreen quality of friendship ('Love and Friendship').

Everyday domestic affection is not usually seen as exciting enough to erupt in colourful poetry, though this subject is sometimes treated by our poets. Unfortunately they seem not to agree on the degree of happiness attainable through quotidian love. It is true that Robert Louis Stevenson aspires to a life of nomadic happiness unspoilt even by the need for cooking and washing ('Romance'), and that James Thomson claims that a man will be happy if he has his pipe and book along with a girl to love ('Gifts'), but these poems are undermined by Stephen Phillips whose spirit returns from beyond the grave only to recall many hours wasted in domestic quarrelling ('The Apparition').

The very darkest side of love, nothing less than evil lust, is depicted in an extract from Lord Macaulay's 'Virginia' (Lays of Ancient Rome). Lucrece is a pretty young girl observed by Appius as she trips home from school; it is painfully certain that all will end in tragedy when we read

> And all along the Forum, and up the Sacred Street,
> His vulture eye pursued the trip of those small glancing feet.

This dark extract from a narrative poem puts into cold perspective all the flippant comments on infidelity dashed off by the other casual lovers, but – thank heaven – there is no suggestion in this collection or in the entire run of English lyric poetry that violent concupiscence is anywhere near the norm of erotic experience.

The Lineaments of Gratified Desire

These thoughts bring us back to sex, which underlies all questions of love. It is only the degree of frankness that varies. William Blake was remarkably forthright on this subject ('The Question Answered'). What do men require from women? The same thing that women require from men – sexual satisfaction, 'The lineaments of gratified desire'. Many other poets have spoken along similar lines. William Cartwright, speaking of finding 'med'cine for the itch', reminds us that when lovers come together soul by soul 'the body is the way'. For him the process is inescapable. Whenever I have climbed from sex to soul, and from soul to thought, he recalls, 'From soul I lighted at the sex agen'. Hence the title of his poem in the mid-seventeenth century, 'No Platonic Love'. As we noted above, Thomas D'Urfey wants to attribute saintliness, divinity to his beloved, but can only do so in terms of 'flesh and blood alone' ('Chloe Divine'). The woman's point of view is put by Thomas Parnell, the singer of whose 'Song' wants the best of both worlds. She will continue to appear like an angel, 'But still be a woman to you'. The most thrilling line in this poem is the highly sensual.

When your love runs in blushes through every vein . . .

Sometimes the poet has to be discreet while wanting to purvey the same message. In these circumstances allegory can be of some help. Robert Browning, brought up in Protestant piety, no stranger to desire and the need to disguise it, tells us of a 'Meeting at Night'. The journey is long and hard but fulfilment lies at the end of it. The two hearts find one another and end up 'beating each to each'; before that the poet has 'gain[ed] the cove with pushing prow' and quenched its speed in slush. Here is a poem that tells of sex without mentioning it by name. Robert Herrick's famous description of Julia's attire, with its unforgettable reference to 'The liquefaction of her clothes' ('Upon Julia's Clothes'), is, of course, really addressed to the lovely body within that causes them to flow so sweetly. A splendid example of overt sexual parallelism is found in John Fletcher's 'My man Thomas'. (Put together the names John and Thomas and you have the subject in hand.) Most of the dialogue in

this brief poem comes from the girl who has invited Thomas to visit
her at night; he announces his arrival and she welcomes him,
indicating where he is to be 'lodged' and using the word 'come' five
times in a ten-word span. Nothing indecent here, of course, though
the full meaning of the encounter is unmistakable. Another way of
dealing with sexual arousal in a decorous manner is to say what did
not happen between the lovers, however narrowly they may have
skirted disaster. Thomas Moore's poignantly named 'Did Not'
brings lips and bodies into close erotic proximity, raises the
temperature unbearably, yet still leaves us with

> . . . lovers, who so nearly erred,
> And yet, who did not.

Seldom can so much have been said in negative terms about the
raging reality of physical passion.

Of course there are some writers, well before the twentieth
century, who throw caution to the winds in these matters and call
spades spades. John Wilmot, Earl of Rochester, is easily the most
outspoken English poet on sexual performances of every kind. In
this collection we have included his wonderful little hymn
addressed by a young girl to her 'Ancient Lover' ('A Song of a
Young Lady to Her Ancient Lover'). She describes what she will do
to restore his 'youthful heat'. It will involve taking hold of

> That nobler part, which but to name
> In our sex would be counted shame . . .

Her reviving hand will soon ensure that this organ shall 'In former
warmth and vigour stand'. No place here for embarrassment or
prudery.

Only slightly less explicit is William Shakespeare in an extract
from his first publication, a tragic narrative poem of 1589, 'Venus
and Adonis'. Venus offers her all to an unresponsive lover:

> I'll be a Park, and thou shalt be my Deer.
> Feed where thou wilt, on Mountain or in Dale;
> > Graze on my Lips, and if those Hills be dry
> > Stray lower, where the pleasant Fountains lie.

This seldom-read poem, which is too long for its own good, contains
much erotic material of this kind.

Our last example of overt sexuality in poetry comes from John

Donne ('Going to Bed'). It is worth waiting for. Urging his lover to prepare for bed, the poet instructs her in the art of undressing, finds the normal response in himself and finally pleads with her to let him start the love-making.

> License my roving hands, and let them go,
> Before, behind, between, above, below.
> O my America! my new-found-land . . .

Here is a clever little piece of literature. Surely love-making demands the use of caressing adjectives, dynamic verbs, and lofty conceits. What shall the ignoble and uninteresting *preposition* do in this company? Here is its moment of greatest glory. The second of these lines, which might claim to be one of the most erotically charged in the English language, consists of improbable ingredients – five prepositions, each one disyllabic and alliterative, mockingly confident and full of the good humour that should never be far away from love itself.

From all the riches of English love poetry we have chosen one hundred works, each by a different poet. For the sake of variety, they have been placed not in chronological order but alphabetically according to the name of the poet.

Love Poems

WILLIAM ALLINGHAM

An Evening

A sunset's mounded cloud;
A diamond evening-star;
Sad blue hills afar;
Love in his shroud.

Scarcely a tear to shed;
Hardly a word to say;
The end of a summer day;
Sweet Love dead.

ANON

Love's Logic

I   HER RESPECTABLE PAPA'S
'My dear, be sensible! Upon my word
This – for a woman even – is absurd;
His income's not a hundred pounds, I know;
He's not worth loving.' – 'But I love him so!'

II   HER MOTHER'S
'You silly child! He is well made and tall;
But looks are far from being all in all.
His social standing's low, his family's low;
He's not worth loving.' – 'And I love him so!'

III   HER ETERNAL FRIEND'S
'Is that he picking up the fallen fan?
My dear, he's such an awkward, ugly man!
You must be certain, pet, to answer "No".
He's not worth loving.' – 'And I love him so!'

IV   HER BROTHER'S
'By Jove! were I a girl – through horrid hap –
I wouldn't have a milk-and-water chap.
The man has not a single spark of "go";
He's not worth loving.' – 'Yet I love him so!'

V   HER OWN
'And were he everything to which I've listened;
Though he were ugly, awkward (and he isn't),
Poor, low-born, and destitute of "go",
He is worth loving, for I love him so!'

MATTHEW ARNOLD

Absence

In this fair stranger's eyes of grey
Thine eyes, my love! I see.
I shiver; for the passing day
Had borne me far from thee.

This is the curse of life! that not
A nobler, calmer train
Of wiser thoughts and feelings blot
Our passions from our brain;

But each day brings its petty dust
Our soon-choked souls to fill,
And we forget because we must
And not because we will.

I struggle towards the light; and ye
Once-long'd-for storms of love!
If with the light ye cannot be,
I bear that ye remove.

I struggle towards the light – but oh
While yet the night is chill,
Upon time's barren, stormy flow,
Stay with me, Marguerite, still!

THOMAS LOVELL BEDDOES

Wolfram's Dirge

If thou wilt ease thine heart
   Of love and all its smart,
      Then sleep, dear, sleep;
And not a sorrow
Hang any tear on your eyelashes;
      Lie still and deep,
   Sad soul, until the sea-wave washes
The rim o' the sun to-morrow,
      In eastern sky.

But wilt thou cure thine heart:
Of love and all its smart,
      Then die, dear, die;
'Tis deeper, sweeter,
   Than on a rose-bank to lie dreaming
      With folded eye;
   And there alone, amid the beaming
Of Love's stars, thou'lt meet her
      In eastern sky.

WILLIAM BLAKE

The Question Answered

What is it men in women do require?
The lineaments of gratified desire.
What is it women do in men require?
The lineaments of gratified desire.

FRANCIS WILLIAM BOURDILLON

'The night has a thousand eyes'

The night has a thousand eyes,
   And the day but one;
Yet the light of the bright world dies
   With the dying sun.

The mind has a thousand eyes,
   And the heart but one;
Yet the light of a whole life dies
   When love is done.

NICHOLAS BRETON

A Report Song in a Dream, Between a Shepherd and His Nymph

Shall we go dance the hay? The hay?
Never pipe could ever play
  Better shepherd's roundelay.

Shall we go sing the song? The song?
Never love did ever wrong:
  Fair maids hold hands all along.

Shall we go learn to woo? To woo?
Never thought came ever to
  Better deed, could better do.

Shall we go learn to kiss? To kiss?
Never heart could ever miss
  Comfort, where true meaning is.

Thus at base they run, they run,
When the sport was scarce begun:
  But I waked, and all was done.

ROBERT BRIDGES

'My delight and thy delight'

My delight and thy delight
Walking, like two angels white,
In the gardens of the night:

My desire and thy desire
Twining to a tongue of fire,
Leaping live, and laughing higher:

Thro' the everlasting strife
In the mystery of life.
Love, from whom the world begun,
Hath the secret of the sun.

Love can tell, and love alone,
Whence the million stars were strewn,
Why each atom knows its own,
How, in spite of woe and death,
Gay is life, and sweet is breath:

This he taught us, this we knew,
Happy in his science true,
Hand in hand as we stood
'Neath the shadows of the wood,
Heart to heart as we lay
In the dawning of the day.

EMILY BRONTË

Love and Friendship

Love is like the wild rose-briar,
Friendship like the holly-tree –
The holly is dark when the rose-briar blooms
But which will bloom most constantly?

The wild rose-briar is sweet in spring,
Its summer blossoms scent the air;
Yet wait till winter comes again,
And who will call the wild-briar fair?

Then, scorn the silly rose-wreath now
And deck thee with the holly's sheen,
That when December blights thy brow
He still may leave thy garland green.

WILLIAM BROOME

The Rosebud

Queen of fragrance, lovely Rose,
The beauties of thy leaves disclose!
– But thou, fair Nymph, thyself survey
In this sweet offspring of a day.
That miracle of face must fail,
Thy charms are sweet, but charms are frail:
Swift as the short-lived flower they fly,
At morn they bloom, at evening die:
Though Sickness yet a while forbears,
Yet Time destroys what Sickness spares:
Now Helen lives alone in fame,
And Cleopatra's but a name:
Time must indent that heavenly brow,
And thou must be what they are now.

ELIZABETH BARRETT BROWNING

'How do I love thee? Let me count the ways'

How do I love thee? Let me count the ways.
I love thee to the depth and breadth and height
My soul can reach, when feeling out of sight
For the ends of Being and ideal Grace.
I love thee to the level of every day's
Most quiet need, by sun and candlelight.
I love thee freely, as men strive for Right;
I love thee purely, as they turn from Praise.
I love thee with the passion put to use
In my old griefs, and with my childhood's faith.
I love thee with a love I seemed to lose
With my lost saints, – I love thee with the breath,
Smiles, tears, of all my life! – and, if God choose,
I shall but love thee better after death.

ROBERT BROWNING

Meeting at Night

The grey sea and the long black land;
And the yellow half-moon large and low;
And the startled little waves that leap
In fiery ringlets from their sleep,
As I gain the cove with pushing prow,
And quench its speed i' the slushy sand.

Then a mile of warm sea-scented beach;
Three fields to cross till a farm appears;
A tap at the pane, the quick sharp scratch
And blue spurt of a lighted match,
And a voice less loud, thro' its joys and fears,
Than the two hearts beating each to each!

THOMAS BURBIDGE

'She bewitched me'

She bewitched me
With such a sweet and genial charm,
I knew not when I wounded was,
And when I found it, hugged the harm.

Down hill; ah yes – down hill, down hill I glide,
But such a hill!
One tapestried fall of meadow pride,
Of ladysmock and daffodil.

How soon, how soon adown a rocky stair,
And slips no longer smooth as they are sweet,
Shall I, with backward-streaming hair,
Outfly my bleeding feet?

ROBERT BURNS

A Red, Red Rose

O my Luve's like a red, red rose,
That's newly sprung in June;
O my Luve's like the melodie
That's sweetly play'd in tune.

As fair art thou, my bonnie lass,
So deep in luve am I:
And I will love thee still, my Dear,
Till a' the seas gang dry.

Till a' the seas gang dry, my Dear,
And the rocks melt wi' the sun;
I will love thee still, my Dear,
While the sands o' life shall run.

And fare thee weel, my only Luve,
And fare thee weel, a while!
And I will come again, my Luve,
Tho' it were ten thousand mile!

LORD GEORGE BYRON

Love

Yes, Love indeed is light from heaven;
    A spark of that immortal fire
With angels shared, by Alla given,
    To lift from earth our low desire.
Devotion wafts the mind above,
But heaven itself descends in love;
A feeling from the Godhead caught,
To wean from self each sordid thought;
A ray of Him who formed the whole;
A glory circling round the soul!

THOMAS CAMPBELL

Freedom and Love

How delicious is the winning
Of a kiss at Love's beginning,
When two mutual hearts are sighing
For the knot there's no untying!

Yet remember, 'midst our wooing
Love has bliss, but Love has ruing;
Other smiles may make you fickle,
Tears for other charms may trickle.

Love he comes, and Love he tarries,
Just as fate our fancy carries;
Longest stays, when sorest chidden;
Laughs and flies, when press'd and bidden.

Bind the sea to slumber stilly,
Bind its odour to the lily,
Bind the aspen ne'er to quiver,
Then bind Love to last forever.

Love's a fire that needs renewal
Of fresh beauty for its fuel:
Love's wing moults when caged and captured,
Only free, he soars enraptured.

Can you keep the bee from ranging
Or the ringdove's neck from changing?
No! nor fetter'd Love from dying
In the knot there's no untying.

THOMAS CAMPION

'There is a garden in her face'

There is a garden in her face,
Where roses and white lilies grow;
A heavenly paradise is that place,
Wherein all pleasant fruits do grow;
There cherries grow that none may buy
Till 'cherry ripe' themselves do cry.

Those cherries fairly do enclose
Of orient pearl a double row,
Which, when her lovely laughter shows,
They look like rosebuds fill'd with snow;
Yet them no peer nor prince may buy
Till 'cherry ripe' themselves do cry.

Her eyes like angels watch them still,
Her brows like bended bows do stand,
Threatening with piercing frowns to kill
All that approach with eye or hand
These sacred cherries to come nigh,
Till 'cherry ripe' themselves do cry.

THOMAS CAREW

Red and White Roses

Read in these Roses the sad story
Of my hard fate, and your owne glory.
In the White you may discover
The paleness of a fainting lover;
In the Red the flames still feeding
On my heart, with fresh wounds bleeding.
The White will tell you how I languish,
And the Red express my anguish;
The White my innocence displaying,
The Red my martyrdom betraying.
The frowns that on your brow resided,
Have those Roses thus divided.
Oh! let your smiles but clear the weather,
And then they both shall grow together.

WILLIAM CARTWRIGHT

No Platonic Love

Tell me no more of minds embracing minds,
And hearts exchang'd for hearts;
That spirits spirits meet, as winds do winds,
And mix their subt'lest parts;
That two unbodied essences may kiss,
And then like angels, twist and feel one bliss.

I was that silly thing that once was wrought
To practise this thin love;
I climb'd from sex to soul, from soul to thought;
But thinking there to move,
Headlong I roll'd from thought to soul, and then
From soul I lighted at the sex agen.

As some strict down-look'd men pretend to fast
Who yet in closets eat;
So lovers who profess they spirits taste,
Feed yet on grosser meat;
I know they boast they souls to souls convey,
Howe'er they meet, the body is the way.

Come, I will undeceive thee, they that tread
Those vain aerial ways,
Are like young heirs and alchymists misled
To waste their wealth and days,
For searching thus to be for ever rich,
They only find a med'cine for the itch.

GEOFFREY CHAUCER

To Rosamounde

A Balade

Madame, ye ben of al beauté shryne
As fer as cercled is the mapemounde,
For as the cristal glorious ye shyne,
And lyke ruby ben your chekes rounde.
Therwith ye ben so mery and so jocounde
That at a revel whan that I see you daunce,
It is an oynement unto my wounde,
Thogh ye to me ne do no daliaunce.

For thogh I wepe of teres ful a tyne,
Yet may that wo myn herte nat confounde;
Your seemly voys, that ye so smal outtwyne,
Maketh my thoght in joye and blis habounde.
So curtaysly I go, with love bounde,
That to myself I sey, in my penaunce,
'Suffyseth me to love you, Rosamounde,
Thogh ye to me ne do no daliaunce.'

Nas never pyk walwed in galauntyne
As I in love am walwed and ywounde,
For which ful ofte I of myself devyne
That I am trewe Tristam the secounde.
My love may not refreyd be nor affounde;
I brenne ay in an amorous plesaunce.
Do what you lyst, I wil your thral be founde,
Thogh ye to me ne do no daliaunce.

JOHN CLARE

'I hid my love . . .'

I hid my love when young till I
Couldn't bear the buzzing of a fly;
I hid my love to my despite
Till I could not bear to look at light:
I dare not gaze upon her face
But left her memory in each place;
Where'er I saw a wild flower lie
I kissed and bade my love good-bye.

I met her in the greenest dells,
Where dewdrops pearl the wood bluebells;
The lost breeze kissed her bright blue eye,
The bee kissed and went singing by,
A sunbeam found a passage there,
A gold chain round her neck so fair;
As secret as the wild bee's song
She lay there all the summer long.

I hid my love in field and town
Till e'en the breeze would knock me down;
The bees seemed singing ballads o'er,
The fly's bass turned a lion's roar;
And even silence found a tongue,
To haunt me all the summer long;
The riddle nature could not prove
Was nothing else but secret love.

HARTLEY COLERIDGE

Early Death

She pass'd away like morning dew
   Before the sun was high;
So brief her time, she scarcely knew
   The meaning of a sigh.

As round the rose its soft perfume,
   Sweet love around her floated;
Admired she grew – while mortal doom
   Crept on, unfear'd, unnoted.

Love was her guardian Angel here,
   But Love to Death resign'd her;
Tho' Love was kind, why should we fear
   But holy Death is kinder?

MARY COLERIDGE

Jealousy

'The myrtle bush grew shady
  Down by the ford.' –
'Is it even so?' said my lady.
  'Even so!' said my lord.
'The leaves are set too thick together
  For the point of a sword.'

'The arras in your room hangs close,
  No light between!
You wedded one of those
  That see unseen.' –
'Is it even so?' said the King's Majesty.
  'Even so!' said the Queen.

SAMUEL TAYLOR COLERIDGE

Answer to a Child's Question

Do you ask what the birds say? The Sparrow, the Dove,
The Linnet and Thrush say, 'I love and I love!'
In the winter they're silent – the wind is so strong;
What it says, I don't know, but it sings a loud song.
But green leaves, and blossoms, and sunny warm weather,
And singing, and loving – all come back together.

But the Lark is so brimful of gladness and love,
The green fields below him, the blue sky above,
That he sings, and he sings; and for ever sings he –
'I love my Love, and my Love loves me!'

WILLIAM CONGREVE

Song

Pious Selinda goes to prayers,
   If I but ask the favour;
And yet the tender fool's in tears,
   When she believes I'll leave her.

Would I were free from this restraint,
   Or else had hopes to win her;
Would she could make of me a saint,
   Or I of her a sinner.

GEORGE CRABBE

A Marriage Ring

The ring so worn as you behold,
So thin, so pale, is yet of gold:
The passion such it was to prove;
Worn with life's cares, love yet was love.

SAMUEL DANIEL

'Love is a sickness . . .'

Love is a sickness full of woes,
    All remedies refusing;
A plant that with most cutting grows,
    Most barren with best using.
          Why so?
More we enjoy it, more it dies;
If not enjoy'd, it sighing cries –
          Heigh ho!

Love is a torment of the mind,
    A tempest everlasting;
And Jove hath made it of a kind
    Not well, nor full nor fasting.
          Why so?
More we enjoy it, more it dies;
If not enjoy'd, it sighing cries –
          Heigh ho!

GEORGE DARLEY

The Solitary Lyre

Wherefore, unlaurell'd Boy,
   Whom the contemptuous Muse will not inspire,
With a sad kind of joy
   Still sing'st thou to thy solitary lyre?

The melancholy winds
   Pour through unnumber'd reeds their idle woes,
And every Naiad finds
   A stream to weep her sorrow as it flows.

Her sighs unto the air
   The Wood-maid's native oak doth broadly tell,
And Echo's fond despair
   Intelligible rocks re-syllable.

Wherefore then should not I,
   Albeit no haughty Muse my heart inspire,
Fated of grief to die,
   Impart it to my solitary lyre?

SIR WILLIAM DAVENANT

'Under the willow-shades . . .'

Under the willow-shades they were
  Free from the eye-sight of the sun,
For no intruding beam could there
  Peep through to spy what things were done:
    Thus sheltered they unseen did lie,
    Surfeiting on each other's eye;
Defended by the willow-shades alone,
The sun's heat they defied and cooled their own.

Whilst they did embrace unspied,
  The conscious willow seemed to smile,
That them with privacy supplied,
  Holding the door, as 't were, the while;
    And when their dalliances were o'er,
    The willows, to oblige them more,
Bowing, did seem to say, as they withdrew,
'We can supply you with a cradle too.'

EMILY DICKINSON

'My life closed twice before its close'

My life closed twice before its close;
　　It yet remains to see
If Immortality unveil
　　A third event to me

So huge, so hopeless to conceive,
　　As these that twice befell.
Parting is all we know of heaven,
　　And all we need of hell.

HENRY AUSTIN DOBSON

Urceus Exit: Triolet

I intended an Ode,
　　And it turn'd to a Sonnet
It began *à la mode*,
I intended an Ode;
But Rose cross'd the road
　　In her latest new bonnet;
I intended an Ode;
　　And it turn'd to a Sonnet.

JOHN DONNE

Going to Bed

Come, Madam, come, all rest my powers defy,
Until I labour, I in labour lie.
The foe oft-times having the foe in sight
Is tired with standing though he never fight.
Off with that girdle, like heaven's zone glittering,
But a far fairer world incompassing.
Unpin that spangled breastplate which you wear,
That th'eyes of busy fools may be stopt there.
Unlace yourself, for that harmonious chime
Tells me from you that now it is bed time.
Off with that happy busk, which I envie,
That still can be, and still can stand so nigh.
Your gown going off such beauteous state reveals
As when from flow'ry meads th'hill's shadow steals.
Off with that wiry coronet and show
The hairy diadem which on you doth grow:
Now off with those shoes, and then safely tread
In this love's hallow'd temple, this soft bed.
In such white robes, heaven's angels us'd to be
Receiv'd by men: thou angel bring'st with thee
A heaven like Mahomet's paradise; and though
Ill spirits walk in white, we easily know
By this these angels from an evil sprite,
Those set our hairs, but these our flesh upright.
    License my roving hands, and let them go,
Before, behind, between, above, below.
O my America! my new-found-land,
My kingdom, safeliest when with one man mann'd,
My mine of precious stones, my emperie,
How blest am I in this discovering thee!
To enter in these bonds, is to be free;
Then where my hand is set, my seal shall be.
    Full nakedness! All joys are due to thee,
As souls unbodied, bodies uncloth'd must be,

To taste whole joys. Gems which you women use
Are like Atlanta's balls, cast in men's views,
That when a fool's eye lighteth on a gem,
His earthly soul may covet theirs, not them.
Like pictures, or like books' gay coverings made
For lay-men, are all women thus array'd;
Themselves are mystic books, which only we
(Whom their imputed grace will dignify)
Must see reveal'd. Then since that I may know,
As liberally, as to a midwife, show
Thy self: cast all, yea, this white linen hence,
There is no penance due to innocence.
   To teach thee, I am naked first; why then
What need'st thou have more covering than a man?

ERNEST DOWSON

Non Sum Qualis Eram Bonae Sub Regno Cynarae

Last night, ah, yesternight, betwixt her lips and mine
There fell thy shadow, Cynara! thy breath was shed
Upon my soul between the kisses and the wine;
And I was desolate and sick of an old passion,
    Yea, I was desolate and bow'd my head:
I have been faithful to thee, Cynara! in my fashion.

All night upon mine heart I felt her warm heart beat,
Night-long within mine arms in love and sleep she lay;
Surely the kisses of her bought red mouth were sweet;
But I was desolate and sick of an old passion,
    When I awoke and found the dawn was gray:
I have been faithful to thee, Cynara! in my fashion.

I have forgot much, Cynara! gone with the wind,
Flung roses, roses, riotously with the throng,
Dancing, to put thy pale lost lilies out of mind;
But I was desolate and sick of an old passion,
    Yea, all the time, because the dance was long:
I have been faithful to thee, Cynara! in my fashion.

I cried for madder music and for stronger wine,
But when the feast is finish'd and the lamps expire,
Then falls thy shadow, Cynara! the night is thine;
And I am desolate and sick of an old passion,
    Yea, hungry for the lips of my desire:
I have been faithful to thee, Cynara! in my fashion.

MICHAEL DRAYTON

'Nothing but no and I, and I and no'

Nothing but no and I, and I and no,
How falls it out so strangely you reply?
I tell ye, fair, I'll not be answered so,
With this affirming no, denying I.
I say, I love, you sleightly answer, I:
I say, you love, you pule me out a no:
I say, I die, you echo me with I:
Save me, I cry, you sigh me out a no;

Must woe and I have nought but no and I?
No I am I, if I no more can have;
Answer no more, with silence make reply,
And let me take myself what I do crave,
   Let no and I, with I and you be so:
   Then answer no and I, and I and no.

JOHN DRYDEN

'Ah, how sweet . . .'

Ah, how sweet it is to love,
Ah, how gay is young desire!
And what pleasing pains we prove
When we first approach Love's fire!
Pains of Love are sweeter far
Than all other pleasures are.

Sighs which are from Lovers blown
Do but gently heave the Heart:
Ev'n the tears they shed alone
Cure, like trickling Balm, their smart.
Lovers, when they lose their breath,
Bleed away in easie death.

Love and Time with reverence use,
Treat 'em like a parting friend:
Nor the golden gifts refuse
Which in youth sincere they send:
For each year their price is more,
And they less simple than before.

Love, like Spring-tides full and high,
Swells in every youthful vein:
But each Tide does less supply,
Till they quite shrink in again.
If a flow in Age appear,
'Tis but rain, and runs not clear.

THOMAS D'URFEY

Chloe Divine

Chloe's a Nymph in flowery groves,
    A Nereid in the streams;
Saint-like she in the temple moves,
    A woman in my dreams.

Love steals artillery from her eyes,
    The Graces point her charms;
Orpheus is rivall'd in her voice,
    And Venus in her arms.

Never so happily in one
    Did heaven and earth combine:
And yet 'tis flesh and blood alone
    That makes her so divine.

SIR GEORGE ETHEREGE

To a Lady Asking Him How Long He Would Love Her

It is not, Celia, in our power
   To say how long our love will last;
It may be we within this hour
   May lose those joys we now do taste;
The Blessèd, that immortal be,
From change in love are only free.

Then since we mortal lovers are,
   Ask not how long our love will last;
But while it does, let us take care
   Each minute be with pleasure past:
Were it not madness to deny
To live because we're sure to die?

JOHN FLETCHER

'My man Thomas'

My man Thomas
Did me promise
He would visit me this night.

I am here, love;
Tell me, dear love,
How I may obtain thy sight.

Come up to my window, love;
Come, come, come:
Come to my window, my dear;
The wind nor the rain
Shall trouble thee again,
But thou shalt be lodged here.

JOHN FORD

'Oh no more, no more, too late'

Oh no more, no more, too late
Sighs are spent; the burning tapers
Of a life as chaste as Fate,
Pure as are unwritten papers,
   Are burnt out: no heat, no light
   Now remains, 'tis ever night.
Love is dead, let lovers' eyes,
   Lock'd in endless dreams,
   Th'extreme of all extremes,
Ope no more, for now Love dies,
   Now Love dies, implying
Love's martyrs must be ever, ever dying.

GEORGE GASCOIGNE

'And if I did what then?'

And if I did what then?
Are you aggriev'd therefore?
The sea hath fish for every man,
And what would you have more?

Thus did my Mistress once,
Amaze my mind with doubt:
And popt a question for the nonce,
To beat my brains about.

Whereto I thus replied,
Each fisherman can wish,
That all the sea at every ride,
Were his alone to fish.

And so did I (in vain),
But since it may not be:
Let such fish there as find the gain,
And leave the loss for me.

And with such luck and loss,
I will content my self:
Till tides of turning time may toss,
Such fishers on the shelf.

And when they stick on sands,
That every man may see:
Then will I laugh and clap my hands,
As they do now at me.

OLIVER GOLDSMITH

Song

When lovely woman stoops to folly,
   And finds too late that men betray,
What charm can soothe her melancholy;
   What art can wash her guilt away?

The only art her guilt to cover,
   To hide her shame from every eye,
To give repentance to her lover,
   And wring his bosom – is to die.

FANNY GREVILLE

Prayer For Indifference

I ask no kind return of love,
　　No tempting charm to please;
Far from the heart those gifts remove,
　　That sighs for peace and ease.

Nor peace nor ease the heart can know,
　　That, like the needle true,
Turns at the touch of joy or woe,
　　But, turning, trembles too.

Far as distress the soul can wound,
　　'Tis pain in each degree:
'Tis bliss but to a certain bound,
　　Beyond is agony.

THOMAS HARDY

The Voice

Woman much missed, how you call to me, call to me,
Saying that now you are not as you were
When you had changed from the one who was all to me,
But as at first, when our day was fair.

Can it be you that I hear? Let me view you, then,
Standing as when I drew near to the town
Where you would wait for me: yes, as I knew you then,
Even to the original air-blue gown!

Or is it only the breeze, in its listlessness
Travelling across the wet mead to me here,
You being ever consigned to existlessness,
Heard no more again far or near?

Thus I: faltering forward,
Leaves around me falling,
Wind oozing thin through the thorn from norward,
And the woman calling.

BRET HARTE

What the Bullet Sang

O joy of creation,
            To be!
O rapture, to fly
            And be free!
Be the battle lost or won,
Though its smoke shall hide the sun,
I shall find my love – the one
            Born for me!

I shall know him where he stands
            All alone,
With the power in his hands
            Not o'erthrown;
I shall know him by his face,
By his godlike front and grace;
I shall hold him for a space
            All my own!

It is he – O my love!
            So bold!
It is I – all thy love
            Foretold!
It is I – O love, what bliss!
Dost thou answer to my kiss?
O sweetheart! what is this
            Lieth there so cold?

GEORGE HERBERT

Love

Love bade me welcome; yet my soul drew back,
    Guilty of dust and sin.
But quick-eyed Love, observing me grow slack
    From my first entrance in,
Drew nearer to me, sweetly questioning,
    If I lack anything.

'A guest,' I answered, 'worthy to be here.'
    Love said, 'You shall be he.'
'I, the unkind, ungrateful! Ah, my dear,
    I cannot look on Thee.'
Love took my hand, and smiling, did reply,
    'Who made the eyes but I?'

'Truth, Lord, but I have marred them; let my shame
    Go where it doth deserve.'
'And know you not,' said Love, 'who bore the blame?'
    'My dear, then I will serve.'
'You must sit down,' said Love, 'and taste my meat.'
    So I did sit and eat.

ROBERT HERRICK

Upon Julia's Clothes

Whenas in silks my Julia goes,
Then, then, methinks, how sweetly flows
The liquefaction of her clothes.

Next, when I cast mine eyes and see
That brave vibration each way free,
O how that glittering taketh me!

THOMAS HOOD

Ruth

Love, see thy lover humbled at thy feet,
Not in servility, but homage sweet,
Gladly inclined: – and with my bended knee
Think that my inward spirit bows to thee –
More proud indeed than when I stand or climb
Elsewhere: – there is no statue so sublime
As Love's in all the world, and e'en to kiss
The pedestal is still a better bliss
Than all ambitions. O! Love's lowest base
Is far above the reaching of disgrace
To shame this posture. Let me then draw nigh
Feet that have fared so nearly to the sky,
And when this duteous homage has been given
I will rise up and clasp the heart in Heaven.

GERARD MANLEY HOPKINS

At the Wedding March

God with honour hang your head,
Groom, and grace you, bride, your bed
With lissome scions, sweet scions,
Out of hallowed bodies bred.

Each be other's comfort kind:
Déep, déeper than divined,
Divine charity, dear charity,
Fast you ever, fast bind.

Then let the march tread our cars:
I to him turn with tears
Who to wedlock, his wonder wedlock,
Déals tríumph and immortal years.

LEIGH HUNT

'Jenny Kiss'd Me . . .'

Jenny kiss'd me when we met,
      Jumping from the chair she sat in;
Time, you thief, who love to get
      Sweets into your list, put that in!
Say I'm weary, say I'm sad,
      Say that health and wealth have miss'd me,
Say I'm growing old, but add,
      Jenny kiss'd me.

RICHARD JAGO

Absence

With leaden foot Time creeps along
   While Delia is away:
With her, nor plaintive was the song,
   Nor tedious was the day.

Ah, envious Pow'r! reverse my doom;
   Now double thy career,
Strain ev'ry nerve, stretch ev'ry plume,
   And rest them when she's here!

BEN JONSON

To Celia

Drink to me only with thine eyes,
And I will pledge with mine;
Or leave a kiss but in the cup
And I'll not look for wine.
The thirst that from the soul doth rise
Doth ask a drink divine;
But might I of Jove's nectar sup
I would not change for thine.

I sent thee late a rosy wreath,
Not so much honouring thee
As giving it a hope, that there
It could not wither'd be;
But thou thereon did'st only breathe
And sent'st it back to me;
Since when it grows, and smells, I swear,
Not of itself, but thee.

JOHN KEATS

The Eve of St Agnes (Extract)

And still she slept an azure-lidded sleep,
In blanched linen, smooth, and lavendered,
While he from forth the closet brought a heap
Of candied apple, quince, and plum, and gourd;
With jellies soother than the creamy curd,
And lucent syrops, tinct with cinnamon;
Manna and dates, in argosy transferred
From Fez; and spiced dainties, every one,
From silken Samarcand to cedared Lebanon.

These delicates he heaped with glowing hand
On golden dishes and in baskets bright
Of wreathed silver: sumptuous they stand
In the retired quiet of the night,
Filling the chilly room with perfume light. –
'And now, my love, my seraph fair, awake!
Thou art my heaven, and I thine eremite:
Open thine eyes, for meek St Agnes' sake,
Or I shall drowse beside thee, so my soul doth ache.'

Thus whispering, his warm, unnerved arm
Sank in her pillow. Shaded was her dream
By the dusk curtains: – 'twas a midnight charm
Impossible to melt as iced stream:
The lustrous salvers in the moonlight gleam;
Broad golden fringe upon the carpet lies:
It seemed he never, never could redeem
From such a stedfast spell his lady's eyes
So mused awhile, entoiled in woofed phantasies.

WALTER SAVAGE LANDOR

'Proud word you never spoke . . .'

Proud word you never spoke, but you will speak
    Four not exempt from pride some future day.
Resting on one white hand a warm wet cheek
    Over my open volume you will say,
      'This man loved *me*!' then rise and trip away.

HENRY WADSWORTH LONGFELLOW

Hiawatha's Wooing (Hiawatha) (Extract)

Yes, as in a dream she listened
To the words of Hiawatha.
As he talked of old Nokomis,
Who had nursed him in his childhood,
As he told of his companions,
Chibiabos, the musician,
And the very strong man, Kwasind,
And of happiness and plenty
In the land of the Ojibways,
In the pleasant land and peaceful.
  'After many years of warfare,
Many years of strife and bloodshed,
There is peace between the Ojibways
And the tribe of the Dacotahs.'
Thus continued Hiawatha,
And then added, speaking slowly,
'That this peace may last for ever,
And our hands be clasped more closely,
And our hearts be more united,
Give me as my wife this maiden,
Minnehaha, Laughing Water,
Loveliest of Dacotah women!'
  And the ancient Arrow-maker
Paused a moment ere he answered,
Smoked a little while in silence,
Looked at Hiawatha proudly,
Fondly looked at Laughing Water,
And made answer, very gravely:
'Yes, if Minnehaha wishes;
Let your heart speak, Minnehaha!'
  And the lovely Laughing Water
Seemed more lovely, as she stood there
Neither willing nor reluctant,
As she went to Hiawatha,

Softly took the seat beside him,
While she said, and blushed to say it,
'I will follow you, my husband!'
   This was Hiawatha's wooing!

RICHARD LOVELACE

To Althea From Prison

When love with unconfinèd wings
   Hovers within my gates,
And my divine Althea brings
   To whisper at my grates;
When I lie tangled in her hair,
   And fettered to her eye,
The birds that wanton in the air
   Know no such liberty.

When flowing cups run swiftly round,
   With no allaying Thames –
Our careless heads with roses bound,
   Our hearts with loyal flames;
When thirsty grief in wine we steep;
   When healths and draughts go free,
Fishes that tipple in the deep
   Know no such liberty.

When, linnet-like confinèd, I
   With shriller throat shall sing
The sweetness, mercy, majesty,
   And glories of my king;
When I shall voice aloud how good
   He is, how great should be,
Enlargèd winds that curl the flood
   Know no such liberty.

Stone walls do not a prison make,
   Nor iron bars a cage;
Minds, innocent and quiet, take
   That for a hermitage:
If I have freedom in my love,
   And in my soul am free; –
Angels alone, that soar above,
   Enjoy such liberty.

JOHN LYLY

Cards and Kisses

Cupid and my Campaspe play'd
At cards for kisses – Cupid paid:
He stakes his quiver, bow, and arrows,
His mother's doves, and team of sparrows;
Loses them too; then down he throws
The coral of his lips, the rose
Growing on's cheek (but none knows how);
With these, the crystal of his brow,
And then the dimple of his chin:
All these did my Campaspe win.
At last he set her both his eyes –
She won, and Cupid blind did rise.
   O Love! has she done this for thee?
   What shall, alas! become of me?

LORD GEORGE LYTTELTON

Tell Me My Heart If This Be Love

When Delia on the plain appears,
Awed by a thousand tender fears,
I would approach, but dare not move; –
Tell me, my heart, if this be love.

Whene'er she speaks, my ravished ear
No other voice than hers can hear,
No other wit but hers approve; –
Tell me, my heart, if this be love.

If she some other swain commend,
Though I was once his fondest friend,
His instant enemy I prove; –
Tell me, my heart, if this be love.

When she is absent, I no more
Delight in all that pleased before –
The clearest spring, the shadiest grove; –
Tell me, my heart, if this be love.

When, fond of power, of beauty vain,
Her nets she spread for every swain,
I strove to hate, but vainly strove; –
Tell me, my heart, if this be love.

LORD THOMAS BABINGTON MACAULAY

Virginia (Lays of Ancient Rome) (Extract)

Just then, as through one cloudless chink in a black stormy sky,
Shines out the dewy morning-star, a fair young girl came by.
With her small tablets in her hand, and her satchel on her arm,
Home she went bounding from the school, nor dreamed of shame
   or harm;
And past those dreaded axes she innocently ran,
With bright, frank brow that had not learned to blush at gaze of
   man;
And up the Sacred Street she turned, and, as she danced along,
She warbled gaily to herself lines of the good old song,
How for a sport the princes came spurring from the camp,
And found Lucrece, combing the fleece, under the midnight
   lamp.
The maiden sang as sings the lark, when up he darts his flight,
From his nest in the green April corn, to meet the morning light;
And Appius heard her sweet young voice, and saw her sweet
   young face,
And loved her with the accursed love of his accursed race,
And all along the Forum, and up the Sacred Street,
His vulture eye pursued the trip of those small glancing feet.

ROBERT MANYNG OF BRUNNE

Praise of Women

No thyng is to man so dere
As wommanys love in gode manerc.
A gode womman is mannys blys,
There here love right and stedfast is.
There is no solas under hevene,
Of alle that a man may nevene,
That shuld a man do so moche glcw
As a gode womman that loveth trew.
Ne derer is none in Goddys hurde
Than a chaste womman with lovely worde.

CHRISTOPHER MARLOWE

The Passionate Shepherd to His Love

Come live with me and be my love,
And we will all the pleasures prove
That valleys, groves, hills and fields,
Or woods or steepy mountain yields.

And we will sit upon the rocks,
And see the shepherds feed their flocks
By shallow rivers, to whose falls
Melodious birds sing madrigals.

And I will make thee beds of roses
And a thousand fragant posies;
A cap of flowers, and a kirtle
Embroidered all with leaves of myrtle.

A gown made of the finest wool
Which from our pretty lambs we pull;
Fair linèd slippers for the cold,
With buckles of the purest gold.

A belt of straw and ivy-buds
With coral clasps and amber studs:
And if these pleasures may thee move,
Come live with me and be my love.

Thy shepherd swains shall dance and sing
For thy delight each May morning:
If these delights thy mind may move,
Then live with me and be my love.

ANDREW MARVELL

An Epitaph

Enough; and leave the rest to Fame!
'Tis to commend her, but to name,
Courtship which, living, she declined,
When dead, to offer were unkind:
Nor can the truest wit, or friend,
Without detracting, her commend.

To say – she lived a virgin chaste
In this age loose and all unlaced;
Nor was, when vice is so allowed,
Of virtue or ashamed or proud;
That her soul was on Heaven so bent,
No minute but it came and went;
That, ready her last debt to pay,
She summ'd her life up every day;
Modest as morn, as mid-day bright,
Gentle as evening, cool as night:
– 'Tis true; but all too weakly said,
'Twas more significant, she's dead.

GEORGE MEREDITH

Love's Grave

Mark where the pressing wind shoots javelin-like,
Its skeleton shadow on the broad-back'd wave!
Here is a fitting spot to dig Love's grave;
Here where the ponderous breakers plunge and strike,
And dart their hissing tongues high up the sand:
In hearing of the ocean, and in sight
Of those ribb'd wind-streaks running into white.
If I the death of Love had deeply plann'd,

I never could have made it half so sure,
As by the unblest kisses which upbraid
The full-waked sense; or failing that, degrade!
'Tis morning: but no morning can restore
What we have forfeited. I see no sin:
The wrong is mix'd. In tragic life, God wot,
No villain need be! Passions spin the plot:
We are betray'd by what is false within.

THOMAS MOORE

Did Not

'Twas a new feeling – something more
Than we had dared to own before,
　　Which then we hid not;
We saw it in each other's eye,
And wished, in every half-breathed sigh,
　　To speak, but did not.

She felt my lips' impassioned touch –
'Twas the first time I dared so much,
　　And yet she chid not;
But whispered o'er my burning brow,
'Oh, do you doubt I love you now?'
　　Sweet soul! I did not.

Warmly I felt her bosom thrill,
I pressed it closer, closer still,
　　Though gently bid not;
Till – oh! the world hath seldom heard
Of lovers, who so nearly erred,
　　And yet, who did not.

WILLIAM MORRIS

'Love is enough . . .'

Love is enough: though the World be a-waning,
And the woods have no voice but the voice of complaining,
  Though the sky be too dark for dim eyes to discover
The gold-cups and daisies fair blooming thereunder,
Though the hills be held shadows, and the sea a dark wonder
  And this day draw a veil over all deeds pass'd over,
Yet their hands shall not tremble, their feet shall not falter;
The void shall not weary, the fear shall not alter
  These lips and these eyes of the loved and the lover.

CAROLINE ELIZABETH SARAH NORTON

'I do not love thee . . .'

I do not love thee! – no! I do not love thee!
And yet when thou art absent I am sad;
   And envy even the bright blue sky above thee,
Whose quiet stars may see thee and be glad.

I do not love thee! – yet, I know not why,
Whate'er thou dost seems still well done, to me:
   And often in my solitude I sigh
That those I do love are not more like thee!

I do not love thee! – yet, when thou art gone,
I hate the sound (though those who speak be dear)
   Which breaks the lingering echo of the tone
Thy voice of music leaves upon my ear.

I do not love thee! – yet thy speaking eyes,
With their deep, bright, and most expressive blue,
   Between me and the midnight heaven arise,
Oftener than any eyes I ever knew.

I know I do not love thee! yet, alas!
Others will scarcely trust my candid heart;
   And oft I catch them smiling as they pass,
Because they see me gazing where thou art.

THOMAS OTWAY

The Enchantment

I did but look and love awhile,
   'Twas but for one half-hour;
Then to resist I had no will,
   And now I have no power.

To sigh and wish is all my ease;
   Sighs which do heat impart
Enough to melt the coldest ice,
   Yet cannot warm your heart.

O would your pity give my heart
   One corner of your breast,
'Twould learn of yours the winning art,
   And quickly steal the rest.

ISOBEL PAGAN

'Ca' the yowes to the knowes'

Ca' the yowes to the knowes,
Ca' them where the heather grows,
Ca' them where the burnie rows,
　　My bonnie dearie.

As I gaed down the water side,
There I met my shepherd lad;
He row'd me sweetly in his plaid,
　　And he ca'd me his dearie.

'Will ye gang down the water side,
And see the waves sae sweetly glide
Beneath the hazels spreading wide?
　　The moon it shines fu' clearly.'

'I was bred up at nae sic school,
My shepherd lad, to play the fool,
And a' the day to sit in dool,
　　And naebody to see me.'

'Ye sall get gowns and ribbons meet,
Cauf-leather shoon upon your feet,
And in my arms ye'se lie and sleep,
　　And ye sall be my dearie.'

'If ye'll but stand to what ye've said,
I'se gang wi' you, my shepherd lad,
And ye may row me in your plaid,
　　And I sall be your dearie.'

'While waters wimple to the sea,
While day blinks in the lift sae hie,
Till clay-cauld dath sall blin' my e'e,
　　Ye aye sall be my dearie!'

THOMAS PARNELL

Song

When thy beauty appears
 In its graces and airs
All bright as an angel new dropp'd from the sky,
At distance I gaze and am awed by my fears:
 So strangely you dazzle my eye!

But when without art
 Your kind thoughts you impart,
When your love runs in blushes through every vein;
When it darts from your eyes, when it pants in your heart,
 Then I know you're a woman again.

There's a passion and pride
 In our sex (she replied),
And thus, might I gratify both, I would do:
Still an angel appear to each lover beside,
 But still be a woman to you.

COVENTRY PATMORE

The Married Lover

Why, having won her, do I woo?
  Because her spirit's vestal grace
Provokes me always to pursue,
  But, spirit-like, eludes embrace;
Because her womanhood is such
  That, as on court-days subjects kiss
The Queen's hand, yet so near a touch
  Affirms no mean familiarness;
Nay, rather marks more fair the height
  Which can with safety so neglect
To dread, as lower ladies might,
  That grace could meet with disrespect;
Thus she with happy favour feeds
  Allegiance from a love so high
That thence no false conceit proceeds
  Of difference bridged, or state put by;

Because although in act and word
  As lowly as a wife can be,
Her manners, when they call me lord,
  Remind me 'tis by courtesy;
Not with her least consent of will,
  Which would my proud affection hurt,
But by the noble style that still
  Imputes an unattain'd desert;
Because her gay and lofty brows,
  When all is won which hope can ask,
Reflect a light of hopeless snows,
  That bright in virgin ether bask;
Because, though free of the outer court
  I am, this Temple keeps its shrine
Sacred to Heaven; because, in short,
  She's not and never can be mine.

GEORGE PEELE

'Hot sun, cool fire, temper'd with sweet air'

Hot sun, cool fire, temper'd with sweet air,
Black shade, fair nurse, shadow my white hair,
Shine, sun, burn, fire, breathe air and ease me,
Black shade, fair nurse, shroud me and please me;
Shadow (my sweet nurse) keep me from burning,
Make not my glad cause, cause of mourning.
Let not my beauty's fire
Enflame unstaid desire,
Nor pierce any bright eye
That wand'reth lightly.

STEPHEN PHILLIPS

The Apparition

My dead Love came to me, and said:
  'God gives me one hour's rest
To spend upon the earth with thee:
  How shall we spend it best?'

'Why, as of old,' I said, and so
  We quarrell'd as of old.
But when I turn'd to make my peace
  That one short hour was told.

EDGAR ALLAN POE

To Helen

Helen, thy beauty is to me
　　Like those Nicèan barks of yore
That gently, o'er a perfumed sea,
　　The weary way-worn wanderer bore
　　To his own native shore.

On desperate seas long wont to roam,
　　Thy hyacinth hair, thy classic face,
Thy Naiad airs have brought me home
　　To the glory that was Greece,
And the grandeur that was Rome.

Lo, in yon brilliant window-niche
　　How statue-like I see thee stand,
　　The agate lamp within thy hand,
Ah! Psyche, from the regions which
　　Are holy land!

ALEXANDER POPE

The Rape of the Lock (Extract)

This nymph, to the destruction of mankind,
Nourished two locks, which graceful hung behind
In equal curls, and well conspired to deck
With shining ringlets the smooth ivory neck.
Love in these labyrinths his slaves detains,
And mighty hearts are held in slender chains.
With hairy springes we the birds betray,
Slight lines of hair surprise the finny prey,
Fair tresses man's imperial race ensnare,
And beauty draws us with a single hair.
Th' advent'rous Baron the bright locks admired;
He saw, he wish'd, and to the prize aspired.
Resolved to win, he meditates the way,
By force to ravish, or by fraud betray;
For when success a lover's toil attends,
Few ask if fraud or force attain'd his ends.

MATTHEW PRIOR

The Lady Who Offers Her Looking-Glass to Venus

Venus, take my votive glass:
Since I am not what I was,
What from this day I shall be,
Venus, let me never see.

SIR WALTER RALEGH

Her Reply

If all the world and love were young,
And truth in every shepherd's tongue,
These pretty pleasures might me move
To live with thee and be thy Love.

But Time drives flocks from field to fold;
When rivers rage and rocks grow cold;
And Philomel becometh dumb;
The rest complains of cares to come.

The flowers do fade, and wanton fields
To wayward Winter reckoning yields:
A honey tongue, a heart of gall,
Is fancy's spring, but sorrow's fall.

Thy gowns, thy shoes, thy beds of roses,
Thy cap, thy kirtle, and thy posies,
Soon break, soon wither – soon forgotten,
In folly ripe, in reason rotten.

Thy belt of straw and ivy-buds,
Thy coral clasps and amber studs, –
All these in me no means can move
To come to thee and be thy Love.

But could youth last, and love still breed,
Had joys no date, nor age no need,
Then these delights my mind might move
To live with thee and be thy Love.

THOMAS RANDOLPH

The Milkmaid's Epithalamium

Joy to the bridegroom and the bride
That lie by one another's side!
O fie upon the virgin beds,
No loss is gain but maidenheads.
Love quickly send the time may be
When I shall deal my rosemary!

I long to simper at a feast,
To dance, and kiss, and do the rest.
When I shall wed, and bedded be
O then the qualm comes over me,
And tells the sweetness of a theme
That I ne'er knew but in a dream.

You ladies have the blessed nights,
I pine in hope of such delights.
And silly damsel only can
Milk the cows' teats and think on man:
And sigh and wish to taste and prove
The wholesome sillabub of love.

Make haste, at once twin-brothers bear;
And leave new matter for a star.
Women and ships are never shown
So fair as when their sails be blown.
Then when the midwife hears your moan,
I'll sigh for grief that I have none.

And you, dear knight, whose every kiss
Reaps the full crop of Cupid's bliss,
Now you have found, confess and tell
That single sheets do make up hell.
And then so charitable be
To get a man to pity me.

CHRISTINA ROSSETTI

Grown and Flown

I loved my love – alas to see
That this should be, alas!
I thought that this could scarcely be,
Yet has it come to pass:
Sweet sweet love was,
Now bitter bitter grown to me.

I loved my love from green of Spring
Until sere Autumn's fall;
But now that leaves are withering
How should one love at all?
One heart's too small
For hunger, cold, love, everything.

I loved my love on sunny days
Until late Summer's wane;
But now that frost begins to glaze
How should one love again?
Nay, love and pain
Walk wide apart in diverse ways.

DANTE GABRIEL ROSSETTI

A Death-Parting

Leaves and rain and the days of the year,
  (*Water-willow and wellaway,*)
All these fall, and my soul gives ear,
And she is hence who once was here.
  (*With a wind blown night and day.*)

Ah! but now, for a secret sign,
  (*The willow's wan and the water white,*)
In the held breath of the day's decline
Her very face seemed pressed to mine.
  (*With a wind blown day and night.*)

O love, of my death my life is fain;
  (*The willows wave on the water-way,*)
Your cheek and mine are cold in the rain,
But warm they'll be when we meet again.
  (*With a wind blown night and day.*)

Mists are heaved and cover the sky;
  (*The willows wail in the waning light,*)
O loose your lips, leave space for a sigh, –
They seal my soul, I cannot die.
  (*With a wind blown day and night.*)

Leaves and rain and the days of the year,
  (*Water-willow and wellaway,*)
All still fall, and I still give ear,
And she is hence, and I am here.
  (*With a wind blown night and day.*)

JOHN RUSKIN

'Trust thou thy Love . . .'

Trust thou thy Love: if she be proud, is she not sweet?
Trust thou thy Love: if she be mute, is she not pure?
Lay thou thy soul full in her hands, low at her feet;
Fail, Sun and Breath! – yet, for thy peace, She shall endure.

CHARLES SACKVILLE, EARL OF DORSET

Dorinda

Dorinda's sparkling wit, and eyes,
    Uniting cast too fierce a light,
Which blazes high, but quickly dies,
    Pains not the heart, but hurts the sight.

Love is a calmer, gentler joy,
    Smooth are his looks and soft his pace,
Her Cupid is a black-guard boy
    That runs his link full in your face.

SIR WALTER SCOTT

The Rover's Adieu

A weary lot is thine, fair maid,
    A weary lot is thine!
To pull the thorn thy brow to braid,
    And press the rue for wine.
A lightsome eye, a soldier's mien,
    A feather of the blue,
A doublet of the Lincoln green –
    No more of me ye knew,
        My Love!
No more of me ye knew.

'This morn is merry June, I trow,
    The rose is budding fain;
But she shall bloom in winter snow
    Ere we two meet again.'
– He turn'd his charger as he spake
    Upon the river shore,
He gave the bridle reins a shake,
    Said 'Adieu for evermore,
        My Love!
And adieu for evermore.'

SIR CHARLES SEDLEY

To Cloris

Cloris, I cannot say your eyes
Did my unwary heart surprise;
Nor will I swear it was your face,
Your shape, or any nameless grace:
For you are so entirely fair,
To love a part, injustice were;
No drowning man can know which drop
Of water his last breath did stop;
So when the stars in heaven appear,
And join to make the night look clear;
The light we no one's bounty call,
But the obliging gift of all.
He that does lips or hands adore;
Deserves them only, and no more;
But I love all, and every part,
And nothing less can ease my heart.
Cupid, that lover, weakly strikes,
Who can express what 'tis he likes.

WILLIAM SHAKESPEARE

Venus and Adonis (Extract)

Sometime she shakes her Head, and then his Hand;
Now gazeth she on him, now on the Ground;
Sometime her Arms enfold him like a Band.
She would, he will not in her Arms be bound;
    And when from thence he struggles to be gone,
    She locks her Lily Fingers one in one.

'Fondling,' she saith, 'Since I have hemm'd thee here
Within the Circuit of this Iv'ry Pale,
I'll be a Park, and thou shalt be my Deer.
Feed where thou wilt, on Mountain or in Dale;
    Graze on my Lips, and if those hills be dry
    Stray lower, where the pleasant Fountains lie.

'Within this Limit is Relief enough,
Sweet Bottom Grass, and high delightful Plain,
Round rising Hillocks, Brakes obscure and rough,
To shelter thee from Tempest and from Rain.
    Then be my Deer, since I am such a Park;
    No Dog shall rouse thee, though a thousand bark.'

JOHN SHEFFIELD, DUKE OF BUCKINGHAMSHIRE

The Reconcilement

Come, let us now resolve at last
　　To live and love in quiet;
We'll tie the knot so very fast
　　That Time shall ne'er untie it.

The truest joys they seldom prove
　　Who free from quarrels live:
'Tis the most tender part of love
　　Each other to forgive.

When least I seem'd concern'd, I took
　　No pleasure nor no rest;
And when I feign'd an angry look,
　　Alas! I loved you best.

Own but the same to me – you'll find
　　How blest will be our fate.
O to be happy – to be kind –
　　Sure never is too late!

PERCY BYSSHE SHELLEY

Love's Philosophy

The fountains mingle with the river,
   And the rivers with the ocean,
The winds of heaven mix for ever
   With a sweet emotion;
Nothing in the world is single;
   All things by a law divine
In one another's being mingle –
   Why not I with thine?

See, the mountains kiss high heaven,
   And the waves clasp one another;
No sister flower would be forgiven
   If it disdained its brother:
And the sunlight clasps the earth,
   And the moonbeams kiss the sea –
What are all these kissings worth
   If thou kiss not me?

JOHN SKELTON

To Mistress Margery Wentworth

With margerain gentle,
   The flower of goodlihead,
Embroidered the mantle
   Is of your maidenhead.
Plainly I cannot glose;
   Ye be, as I divine,
The pretty primrose,
   The goodly columbine.

Benign, courteous, and meek,
   With wordes well devised;
In you, who list to seek,
   Be virtues well comprised.
With margerain gentle,
   The flower of goodlihead,
Embroidered the mantle
   Is of your maidenhead.

ROBERT SOUTHEY

Love Cannot Die

They sin who tell that love can die:
With life all other passions fly,
All others are but vanity.
In heaven ambition cannot dwell,
Nor avarice in the vaults of hell:
Earthly these passions, as of earth,
They perish where they have their birth.
  But Love is indestructible;
Its holy flame for ever burneth,
From heaven it came, to heaven returneth.
Too oft on earth a troubled guest,
At times deceived, at times opprest;
  It here is tried and purified,
And hath in heaven its perfect rest;
It soweth here with toil and care,
But the harvest-time of love is there.
Oh! when a mother meets on high
The babe she lost in infancy,
Hath she not then for pains and fears,
  The day of woe, the anxious night,
For all her sorrow, all her tears,
  An over-payment of delight?

THOMAS STANLEY

The Relapse

O turn away those cruel eyes,
    The stars of my undoing!
Or death, in such a bright disguise,
    May tempt a second wooing.

Punish their blind and impious pride,
    Who dare contemn thy glory;
It was my fall that deified
    Thy name, and seal'd thy story.

Yet no new sufferings can prepare
    A higher praise to crown thee;
Though my first death proclaim thee fair,
    My second will unthrone thee.

Lovers will doubt thou canst entice
    No other for thy fuel,
And if thou burn one victim twice,
    Both think thee poor and cruel.

ROBERT LOUIS STEVENSON

Romance

I will make you brooches and toys for your delight
Of bird-song at morning and star-shine at night.
I will make a palace fit for you and me,
Of green days in forests and blue days at sea.

I will make my kitchen, and you shall keep your room,
Where white flows the river and bright blows the broom,
And you shall wash your linen and keep your body white
In rainfall at morning and dewfall at night.

And this shall be for music when no one else is near,
The fine song for singing, the rare song to hear!
That only I remember, that only you admire,
Of the broad road that stretches and the roadside fire.

WILLIAM STRODE

Chloris in the Snow

I saw fair Chloris walk alone,
When feather'd rain came softly down,
As Jove descending from his Tower
To court her in a silver shower:

The wanton snow flew to her breast,
Like pretty birds into their nest,
But, overcome with whiteness there,
For grief it thaw'd into a tear:
      Thence falling on her garments' hem,
      To deck her, froze into a gem.

SIR JOHN SUCKLING

The Constant Lover

Out upon it, I have loved
   Three whole days together!
And am like to love three more,
   If it prove fair weather.

Time shall moult away his wings
   Ere he shall discover
In the whole wide world again
   Such a constant lover.

But the spite on 't is, no praise
   Is due at all to me:
Love with me had made no stays,
   Had it any been but she.

Had it any been but she,
   And that very face,
There had been at least ere this
   A dozen dozen in her place.

ALGERNON SWINBURNE

The Lute and the Lyre

Deep desire, that pierces heart and spirit to the root,
Finds reluctant voice in verse that yearns like soaring fire,
Takes exultant voice when music holds in high pursuit
     Deep desire.

Keen as burns the passion of the rose whose buds respire,
Strong as grows the yearning of the blossom toward the fruit,
Sounds the secret half unspoken ere the deep tones tire.

Slow subsides the rapture that possessed love's flower-soft lute,
Slow the palpitation of the triumph of the lyre:
Still the soul feels burn, a flame unslaked though these be mute.
     Deep desire.

ALFRED, LORD TENNYSON

Marriage Morning

Light, so low upon earth,
    You send a flash to the sun.
Here is the golden close of love,
    All my wooing is done.
Oh, the woods and the meadows,
    Woods where we hid from the wet,
Stiles where we stay'd to be kind,
    Meadows in which we met!

Light, so low in the vale
    You flash and lighten afar,
For this is the golden morning of love,
    And you are his morning star.
Flash, I am coming, I come,
    By meadow and stile and wood,
Oh, lighten into my eyes and heart,
    Into my heart and my blood!

Heart, are you great enough
    For a love that never tires?
O heart, are you great enough for love?
    I have heard of thorns and briers.
Over the thorns and briers,
    Over the meadows and stiles,
Over the world to the end of it
    Flash for a million miles.

WILLIAM MAKEPEACE THACKERAY

Sorrows of Werther

Werther had a love for Charlotte
   Such as words could never utter;
Would you know how first he met her?
   She was cutting bread and butter.

Charlotte was a married lady,
   And a moral man was Werther,
And, for all the wealth of Indies,
   Would do nothing for to hurt her.

So he sighed and pined and ogled,
   And his passion boiled and bubbled,
Till he blew his silly brains out,
   And no more was by it troubled.

Charlotte, having seen his body
   Borne before her on a shutter,
Like a well-conducted person,
   Went on cutting bread and butter.

JAMES THOMSON

Gifts

Give a man a horse he can ride,
   Give a man a boat he can sail;
And his rank and wealth, his strength and health,
   On sea nor shore shall fail.

Give a man a pipe he can smoke,
   Give a man a book he can read:
And his home is bright with a calm delight,
   Though the room be poor indeed.

Give a man a girl he can love,
   As I, O my love, love thee;
And his heart is great with the pulse of Fate,
   At home, on land, on sea.

WILLIAM WALSH

Rivals

Of all the torments, all the cares,
    With which our lives are curst;
Of all the plagues a lover bears,
    Sure rivals are the worst!
By partners in each other kind
    Afflictions easier grow;
In love alone we hate to find
    Companions of our woe.

Sylvia, for all the pangs you see
    Are labouring in my breast,
I beg not you would favour me,
    Would you but slight the rest!
How great soe'er your rigours are,
    With them alone I'll cope;
I can endure my own despair,
    But not another's hope.

WALT WHITMAN

The Imprisoned Soul

At the last, tenderly,
From the walls of the powerful, fortress'd house,
From the clasp of the knitted locks – from the keep of the well-
    closed doors,
Let me be wafted.

Let me glide noiselessly forth;
With the key of softness unlock the locks – with a whisper
Set ope the doors, O soul!

JOHN WILMOT, EARL OF ROCHESTER

A Song of a Young Lady to Her Ancient Lover

Ancient person, for whom I
All the flattering youth defy,
Long be it ere thou grow old,
Aching, shaking, crazy, cold;
    But still continue as thou art,
    Ancient person of my heart.

On thy withered lips and dry,
Which like barren furrows lie,
Brooding kisses I will pour
Shall thy youthful heat restore
(Such kind showers in autumn fall,
And a second spring recall);
    Nor from thee will ever part,
    Ancient person of my heart.

The nobler part, which but to name
In our sex would be counted shame,
By age's frozen grasp possessed,
From his ice shall be released,
And soothed by my reviving hand,
In former warmth and vigour stand.
All a lover's wish can reach
For thy joy my love shall teach,
And for thy pleasure shall improve
All that art can add to love.
    Yet still I love thee without art,
    Ancient person of my heart.

WILLIAM WORDSWORTH

'She dwelt among the untrodden ways'

She dwelt among the untrodden ways
   Beside the springs of Dove,
A Maid whom there were none to praise
   And very few to love:

A violet by a mossy stone
   Half hidden from the eye!
Fair as a star, when only one
   Is shining in the sky.

She lived unknown, and few could know
   When Lucy ceased to be;
But she is in her grave, and, oh,
   The difference to me!

SIR THOMAS WYATT

'Quondam was I in my lady's grace'

Quondam was I in my lady's grace,
I think as well as now be you;
And when that you have trad the trace,
Then shall you know my words be true,
    That quondam was I.

Quondam was I. She said for ever:
That lasted but a short while;
Promise made not to dissever.
I thought she laugh'd – she did but smile,
    Then quondam was I.

Quondam was I: he that full oft lay
In her arms with kisses many one.
It is enough that this I may say,
Though among the moo now I be gone,
    Yet quondam was I.

Quondam was I. Yet she will you tell
That since the hour she was first born
She never loved none half so well
As you. But what altho she had sworn,
    Sure quondam was I.

Index of Titles or First Lines

Acknowledgements

The editor and publishers would like to thank the following for permission to reproduce copyright material:

Harvard University Press and the Trustees of Amherst College for 'My life closed twice' from *The Poems of Emily Dickinson*, ed. Ralph W Franklin, The Belknap Press of Harvard University Press. Copyright © 1998 by the President and Fellows of Harvard College. Copyright © 1951, 1955, 1979 by the President and Fellows of Harvard College.

Every effort has been made to trace all the copyright holders, but if any have been inadvertently overlooked the publishers will be pleased to make the necessary arrangement at the first opportunity.